The QUICK EXPERT'S GUIDE TO

Computing & Programming

Shahneila Saeed

WAYLAND
www.waylandbooks.co.uk

First published in paperback in 2016 by Wayland

Copyright © Wayland 2016

Wayland
An imprint of
Hachette Children's Group
Part of Hodder & Stoughton
Carmelite House
50 Victoria Embankment
London EC4Y 0DZ

Editor: Hayley Fairhead
Consultant: Chris Martin
Design: Rocket Design (East Anglia) Ltd
All images and graphic elements: Shutterstock

Dewey classification number: 004—dc23

ISBN: 978 0 7502 9777 6
Library ebook ISBN: 978 0 7502 9277 1
10 9 8 7 6 5 4 3 2 1

Printed in China

An Hachette UK company
www.hachette.co.uk
www.hachettechildrens.co.uk

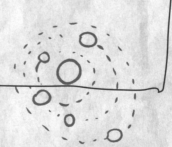

>>>CONTENTS<<<

We have highlighted blogs, websites and tools throughout this guide in bold; we didn't want to overload you with URLs, but you should be able to find them really easily through search engines.

WELCOME >> << TO THE UTTERLY EXCELLENT WORLD OF COMPUTING & PROGRAMMING

Have you ever played a computer game and then wondered how it was made? Are you a gaming whizz with a taste for all things techie?

Today's computer games are amazing! Whether they are on your smartphone, laptop or games console, there's such a huge range. You have the ones that are easy to play and only require a single well-placed tap of your finger, and others which are far more complex and require special hand-held controllers with careful strategic thinking and skill in order to succeed. Whatever the game, no matter how simple or complex; somebody at some point sat down and programmed it into existence.

Programming is a wonderful thing. It's a tool that you can use to create new technologies. Everything you use on the computer is a computer program and has probably required a team of programmers to spend hours developing it.

So, do you fancy making some of your own computer magic? By the time the QEG team has finished with you, you'll be a programming genius!

SO GET READY TO DON YOUR CODING CAP AND SUMMON YOUR CREATIVE KARMA FOR THE QUICK EXPERT TEAM'S SHOW-AND-TELL ON:

How to **talk and think** like a programmer

The people who made **millions** through programming

Making your own **games**

Being a **creative** and **innovative** computer whizz

Learning the programming **language** of **Python**

Chapter 1

ALL ABOUT COMPUTING & PROGRAMMING

✳ WHAT IS COMPUTING AND PROGRAMMING?

Computing is the study of computers and computer systems, and how they work. A dictionary definition refers to it as 'to determine by calculation; reckon; calculate'. Computing as a subject explores the principles and ideas that form the foundation of the activity. So, for example, computing is more concerned with what the World Wide Web and the internet is, how it works and the techniques for searching it rather than how to word process a professional business letter. Computing includes: designing and developing hardware and software, managing information and making computers behave intelligently. However, computers are just machines, and machines need instructions in order to operate; and that's where programming comes in.

Programming is the means by which we give computers the instructions to behave intelligently. If you have a good understanding of the subject you can create some great innovations. For example, the latest iPhone, Smart Watches, wearable technology — including Google Glass, or Smart TVs; they are all computers and they were all created by computer scientists!

✳ HOW IT ALL BEGAN

Computing as a subject is actually a lot older than you might think. It is widely agreed that the first device to carry out any computation was the abacus. The first known abacus was used in 2400 BC by the Babylonians and was made using sand and pebbles!

However, the modern computer wasn't designed until the nineteenth century. In 1837, Charles Babbage wrote about his analytical engine, which had expandable memory, an arithmetic logic unit and processing capabilities to be able to interpret a programming language with repetition (i.e. repeating a certain set of instructions) and conditional branches (e.g. IF Statements, see page 34). Although this machine was never created, Charles Babbage is regarded as one of the first pioneers of computing.

✳ COMPUTERS TODAY

Early computers had their own dedicated programming. So, in order to tell a computer what to do, you had to enter instructions that were specifically tailored for that computer alone.

In 1952, Grace Hopper created the first machine-independent programming language, which led to the development of COBOL. COBOL was one of the first programming languages ever invented. It meant that you could write a computer program on one machine and then transfer it to another. It also meant that computers could do much more than just mathematical calculations.

Grace Hopper believed that computer programs should be written in a language form close to English, rather than in machine code (as had been done previously).

✳ WHAT IS BINARY?

Binary is a number system, using 1s and 0s, which is used by computers to process data. Computers are electrical machines and ultimately they have to make sense of the electrical signals flowing through them.

Think of a light switch: the light bulb only comes on when the switch is on; and that happens because the switch allows electricity to flow through the circuit to reach the bulb. So, let's represent the light bulb being on with a '1' and when the light bulb is off we represent this with a '0'. Now that we've established that, we can choose a series of 1s and 0s to represent whatever we choose. You can work out a secret code that allows you to communicate with another person, just by using the pattern of your light being on and off.

So why talk about the light switch? Well, computers contain millions of electronic switches that work in the same way. When a switch is on it is represented by 1 and when the switch is off it is represented by 0. So using this pattern of on and off switches we can represent everything we ever store inside a computer. Yes, that includes everything from your music collection, to family photos or your favourite film!

So, for example, the words 'Quick Expert' would look something like this in binary:

Character	Q	u	i	c	k	(space)	E	x	p	e	r	t
Binary	01010001	01110101	01101001	01100011	01101011	00100000	01000101	01111000	01110000	01100101	01110010	01110100

WHAT IS HEXADECIMAL?

All those binary 1s and 0s are difficult to read and a little mind boggling. So, machine code was often written using the simpler hexadecimal number system. But how do we get from binary to hexadecimal? Stick with us and all will be revealed.

Binary is a base-2 number system i.e. it only has two values: 1 and 0. Each position is multiplied by 2. In school we are taught a base-10 number system (referred to as denary or decimal); each position is multiplied by 10 and we have 10 different digits, values 0-9. Well, in binary the positions are 1, 2, 4, 8, 16 etc. and the values are 0-1.

Hexadecimal is a base-16 number system i.e. it has 16 values: 0-15. However, because we can only represent 0-9 using our numeric characters, values 10-15 are represented by the letters a-f.

So, for example, the words 'Quick Expert' would look something like this in hexadecimal:

Character	Q	u	i	c	k	(space)	E	x	p	e	r	t
Hexadecimal	51	75	69	63	6b	20	45	78	70	65	72	74

✳ PROGRAMMING IS CREATIVE

Programming is essentially a creative activity. No really, it is! Some of the best technological innovations to date are essentially due to someone thinking 'outside the box' and then applying some computational thinking to it. Computer scientists identify a real world problem and then try to solve it by applying computational thinking. Programming is simply a tool that helps them do this. The important thing is to always identify what you want to do first. Consider your problem and what you are trying to solve. Your problem can usually be broken down into smaller, more manageable parts. For example, take a simple day-to-day issue.

The problem: 'I want to eat some cherries'.

A programmer would be able to use this flowchart to see if things need to be broken down further. For example, 'Wear appropriate clothes' — what does that mean? We could break it down into more detail, where we check the weather to see if we need an umbrella or a sun hat, for example. A programmer would continue to break down the elements of the problem until it couldn't be broken down any more. They would then tackle each sub-problem individually. Once all the sub-problems have been solved, you end up solving the entire problem!

REALITY CHECK

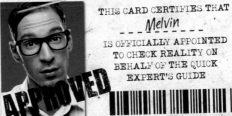

OFFICIAL REALITY CHECKER

THIS CARD CERTIFIES THAT
Melvin
IS OFFICIALLY APPOINTED
TO CHECK REALITY ON
BEHALF OF THE QUICK
EXPERT'S GUIDE

APPROVED

☑ Jan Koum and Brian Acton — WhatsApp Founders

Jan taught himself computer networking by the age of 18, reading manuals he bought at a used book store! He joined Yahoo Inc. as an Infrastructure Engineer, where he met Brian Acton. In 2007, after becoming disillusioned with the way internet companies focused primarily on advertising, the two friends left Yahoo Inc.

In 2009, Jan bought an iPhone and thought that a simple hassle-free instant messaging app would work wonders across the globe to get users to network on a single platform. So he sat down with Brian and programmed his solution. Voila, WhatsApp was born!

By 2011, WhatsApp was in the top 20 apps in the US. By 2014, WhatsApp had amassed over 450 million monthly users. More than 1 million people sign up for WhatsApp every day. In February 2014, Facebook announced its latest acquisition: it had purchased WhatsApp for $19bn. It's safe to say that some creative programming turned Jan and Brian into billionaires!

✳ SO, WHAT ARE ALGORITHMS THEN?

An algorithm is a set of steps taken to solve a problem. A mathematical example of this might be the step-by-step procedure used to carry out long division. For instance, the algorithm for dividing 73 by 3 using long division is:

1. How many times does 3 go into 7? 2

2. How many are left over? 1

3. Put the 1 in front of the 3 (from the original 73): 13

4. How many times does 3 go into 13? 4 with a remainder of 1

5. The answer becomes 24 with a remainder of 1.

Don't fall asleep at the back...!

✳ ALGORITHMS ARE EVERYWHERE!

Algorithms exist everywhere. Given the fact that they refer to a series of steps to solve a problem, you realise that you probably write or follow many algorithms every day. Don't believe us? Well, consider these examples:

🌀 Chefs write algorithms all the time when they write the recipes for their wonderful dishes. A recipe is an algorithm, as it outlines the steps you need to take to recreate the dish.

🌀 Have you ever had to help someone assemble some flat-pack furniture? Well, if you did, the chances are you used an instruction guide full of diagrams. That guide was an algorithm. Algorithms don't have to be just written text, they can be represented easily as diagrams and images whenever appropriate.

Think about your PE lessons when your teacher tells you how to play a new sport. The rules you follow or the steps you take to play the game are an algorithm.

If you follow a sheet of music to play your favourite song on an instrument, the sheet of music is the algorithm that tells you which notes to play.

So, algorithmic thinking is a skill that we can find in all aspects of our life.

Algorithmic thinking is a key part of computing. In fact, programming is how we implement algorithmic thinking. When you write a program, you are simply writing out a set of instructions for the computer, enabling it to solve a problem. Whether that problem is a game, or checking the weather, or organising your music playlist; they all come down to the same thing and that's writing a set of instructions to solve a problem.

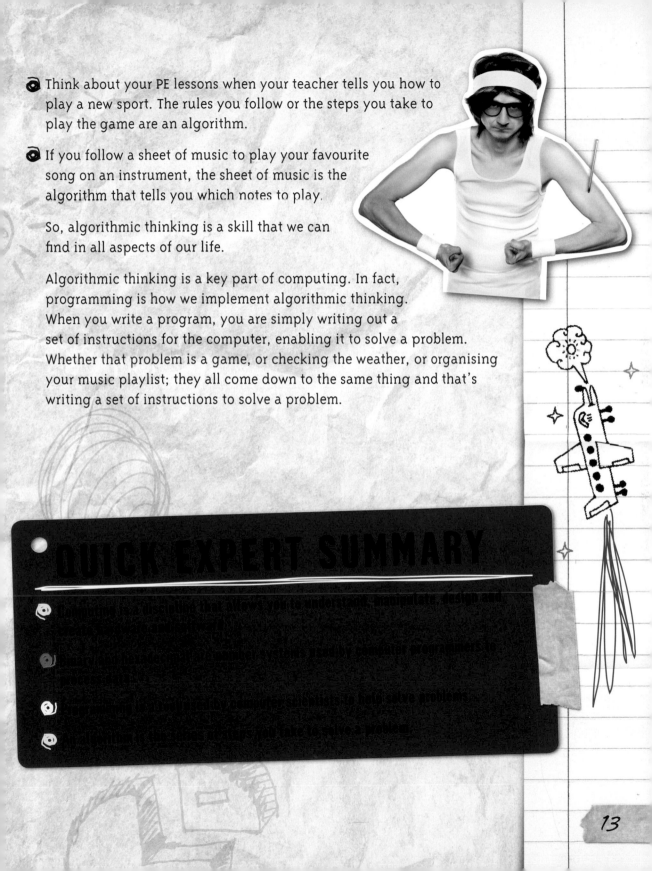

QUICK EXPERT SUMMARY

- Computing is a discipline that allows you to understand, manipulate, design and [illegible]
- [illegible] really computer programmers [illegible]
- [illegible] computer scientists to help solve problems
- Algorithms are the logical steps you take to solve a problem

GETTING TO KNOW PYTHON

* THE LANGUAGE OF PROGRAMMING

There are a number of different programming languages (environments) available for use. Some of these, such as Scratch, Kodu and Greenfoot, are visual programming environments and are designed to teach programming concepts to students. Others are text-based environments and are used both in education and industry. These include Java, C+, JavaScript, Visual Basic, Delphi, Python and many, many more.

In this book, you will be learning how to use the popular programming language Python. Python is a simple yet powerful programming language that will enable you to solve a vast array of potential 'problems'. It's open source, which means it is free to use. Python is used successfully in thousands of applications around the world, such as YouTube, Dropbox and in air traffic control systems.

https://www.python.org

* THE VERSIONS

There are numerous versions of Python. In this book we will be using Version 3.4.1 which can be downloaded from **https://www.python.org/downloads/release/python-341/** You will need to download the version that is most applicable to your computer.

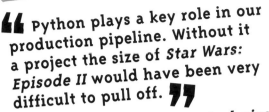

> **"** Python plays a key role in our production pipeline. Without it a project the size of *Star Wars: Episode II* would have been very difficult to pull off. **"**
>
> *Tommy Burnette, Senior Technical Director at visual effects company, Industrial Light and Magic* ←

www.ilm.com

There are different installers for Mac and Windows, so you will need to select appropriately. If you need help choosing which version to download, try the online help guide: **https://wiki.python.org/moin/BeginnersGuide/Download**

When downloaded, it can appear as if Python comes with a lot of additional files, and it can be difficult to understand where to begin or how to make sense of it all. So, before you get stuck in with your first program you need to familiarise yourself with the environment. First things first, turn off your mobile phone, get some doughnuts, pour yourself a drink and find a comfy chair. Ready? Now fire up your computer and spend some time exploring Python and the files you downloaded. Get to know the development environment a little better before you begin to use it.

※ THE ENVIRONMENT AND THE EDITOR

When you explore your Python folder, you'll see four main files in your menu options:

1. IDLE (Python GUI) — this is known as the interactive 'shell' environment. This is the file you want to open to begin your programming and it is where you will write a lot of your code.

2. Module Docs — simply a list of the installed modules that you can import into and use when programming in Python. Don't worry about what a 'module' is just yet, we'll come back to that later (see page 42).

3. Python (Command Line) — a command line interface (where you interact with the computer just by entering instructions or commands i.e. no graphics) for your programming. In your early days you can pretty much ignore this, but as you become more advanced and move on from this book, you may find it useful to switch to this interface to customise and run your programs.

4. Python Manuals — your help files!

Let's begin by exploring the main Python editor that we will be using throughout this book. From your menu, open Python by selecting the icon labelled 'IDLE'.

We can enter commands directly into the shell (which we can refer to as the console). The line that starts with >>> is where Python expects to see your instructions. It will print the results in the line below. So, try something simple, like adding 2+2. It will return the answer '4' on the line below:

```
>>> 2+2

4

>>>
```

Try doing a range of calculations in the shell. Just remember to use the following symbols:

* for multiplication
/ for division
+ for addition
- for subtraction

For example:

```
>>> 20/2
>>> 3*7
>>> 50-5
```

DIY DUDE

Simple maths in Python

Dude!

>> THE BOFFIN BIT <<

UNDERSTANDING SOME KEY TERMS IN PYTHON

The shell environment

The Python shell is an environment where you can enter your code. When you select and open the Python IDLE you will first be provided with a window labelled 'Python 3.4.1 Shell'. Any commands entered here are executed immediately.

Input line

Starts with >>> It's the line where you enter your commands, or 'inputs'.

Print line

The line (s) where Python will display the results of your inputs/commands.

✳ WORKING WITH TEXT

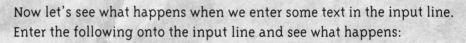

Now let's see what happens when we enter some text in the input line. Enter the following onto the input line and see what happens:

```
>>> print ('Hello World')
```

Python is case sensitive, so capital letters, and where you use them, are important. The command 'print' must be in lower case and this simply tells the computer what to output onto screen. If you are adding text (string), the characters need to be surrounded by brackets and quotation marks. The computer will accept either single or double quotation marks. If you're adding numbers you don't need brackets or quotation marks.

>> THE BOFFIN BIT <<

WHAT DOES 'SYNTAX' MEAN?

The word 'syntax' refers to the structure of text statements in a computer programming language. When you have a syntax error, it usually means you have typed in something incorrectly. For example, in Python this would refer to a missing bracket or a capital letter where you don't need one. A logical error usually refers to mistakes in the 'logic' of your programming code. These errors may not cause your computer program to 'crash' in the same way, but instead the program won't produce the outputs or results that you wanted.

Try entering each of these statements in the input line and see what happens:

1. >>> print ('****************')

2. >>> print 54321

3. >>> 54321

4. >>> print ('123456')

5. >>> 5+4

Dude!

- Statement 1: will print a row of asterisks because you've used brackets and quotation marks.

- Statement 2: will generate a syntax error because, by adding the word 'print', it thinks you're trying to enter text and have forgotten the brackets and quotation marks.

- Statement 3: will print the numbers as you've entered them.

- Statement 4: will also print the numbers as you've entered them. However, these numbers are being treated as text rather than a numerical value. So if you wanted to carry out any calculations using these numbers, you would need to take them out of brackets and quotation marks, and remove the word 'print'.

- Statement 5: will print the result of the calculation.

QUICK EXPERT SUMMARY

PLANNING YOUR GAME

* COMING UP WITH AN IDEA

So, the million dollar question is 'How do we come up with a game idea in the first place?' Well, the key here is to look around you. Think of things you are interested in. For example, what type of games do you enjoy playing? What do you like about them in particular? Brainstorm a bunch of ideas and see which one you like the most.

For your first attempt, try to keep it simple. As you start out in the world of programming it's much better to begin by solving simple problems, or by creating very simple games, until you have developed enough skills to be able to move on to more challenging ideas. For example, one simple game idea is 'Catch the Clown' — a clown randomly moves around the screen and you have to catch it by tapping it or clicking on it.

* WHY IS IT IMPORTANT TO PLAN?

Now you have a super idea for a program and you can't wait to begin creating it. But, stop! Don't rush into it blindly; it's far better to spend some time planning first. Good planning is the key to success. Professional programmers will always spend a good deal of time planning their programs before they actually begin writing them. Professional programs can become quite complex, and because multiple people can be working on one program at the same time it is important that everyone knows what they are supposed to be doing.

You might have a great idea, but then get stuck during the implementation because you don't know where to begin. Having your general idea isn't enough. It is important to break it down into specific jobs or tasks that your program needs to carry out. There are many ways this can be done (including simply writing it out as a list or a brainstorm) but most programmers use the top-down approach.

✳ THE TOP-DOWN APPROACH

The top-down approach is often used to solve computing problems. It simply means that you take your overall idea and then continue to break it down into smaller parts until you can't break it up anymore. Then, when solving the problem, you tackle each sub-problem individually, and in doing so you gradually solve the entire problem. For example, take a simple quiz program. It may require the following functions:

1. Display a question on screen i.e. 2+2= ?

2. Prompt the user for an answer and store it

3. Calculate the correct answer to the question

4. Decide if the user's answer is correct

5. Decide what to do when the answer is correct i.e. increase life/score

6. Decide what to do when the answer is incorrect i.e. decrease life/ score.

This appoach gives a clear idea of what needs to be done to implement the game.

REALITY CHECK

OFFICIAL REALITY CHECKER

THIS CARD CERTIFIES THAT
Melvin
IS OFFICIALLY APPOINTED
TO CHECK REALITY ON
BEHALF OF THE QUICK
EXPERT'S GUIDE

APPROVED

☑ Dong Nguyen
Creator of Flappy Bird

In April 2013, Nguyen, a quiet 28-year-old, spent a holiday weekend making a game for mobile phones. His intention was to create a simple but challenging game that everyone could play and he kept the graphics in line with the Nintendo games he loved to play when he was growing up. And so, 'Flappy Bird' was born.

Nguyen had taught himself how to program after being inspired by Nintendo and Super Mario Bros, and by the age of 16 he had created his own computer chess game. Why did he create 'Flappy Bird'? He became fascinated with the possibilities that touch-screen phones bring and was tired of games with graphics that looked too 'busy'.

Five months after its release, a simple post on Twitter caused the game to go viral. By January 2014, it had hit number 1 on both iTunes and the Google Play store. Nguyen was making an estimated $50,000 a day from in-game advertising. By February, the mania that was 'Flappy Bird' became too much for him, so he withdrew the game. Now phones that still have the original game installed are being sold for thousands on eBay!

OFFICIAL FORM C-185/A

✳ FLOWCHARTS

Another way to represent this problem is by using a flowchart. Diamond shapes represent a decision box within a flowchart. For our quiz example, the flowchart may look like this:

In the previous example, the program continues until all lives have been lost. That may be the way you want your game to work, or you may wish to add alternative ways to end the program. The important thing is that a flowchart like this can help you see exactly how your program is going to run. It's easier to see where the end points are and you can follow the logic to see if you have incorporated all the functions.

For a simple program, one flowchart is usually enough, however, flowcharts can be separated in order to make them clearer to read. This is especially true for more complex programs, which may contain many procedures and functions. Drawing out aspects of your code like this can help you see clearly what you need to do and where you need to begin!

✳ WRITING PSEUDO CODE

You can take your planning one step further. Pseudo code is your program written in plain structured English. It is usually done as part of the design and planning process and it gives you a strong idea of how you might want to organise your code. You can try to convert your flowchart into structured English. For our quiz example, the pseudo code for the flowchart may look like this:

Repeat Until Lives = 0

Retrieve the next question

Print question to screen

Prompt user for answer

Store user's answer in UserAnswer variable

Calculate answer to question

Store calculated answer in CompAnswer variable

If UserAnswer = CompAnswer then

Score = Score + 1

Next question

Else

Lives = Lives -1

When broken down to this level, pseudo code begins to look very similar to actual programming syntax. In fact your pseudo code is actually just an algorithm (see pages 12–13).

Having your ideas written down to pseudo code level can help a great deal when it comes to developing the actual program. Looking at the above pseudo code, we can easily begin to see what syntax we might use in our program.

Remember, one person's pseudo code may vary from another's. The important thing is that the flowchart and the pseudo code work logically and make sense. If you are working on this with a friend, then it is possible to compare your work with theirs. Perhaps you can compare the efficiency of your algorithms.

* COMPLEX GAMES

The key thing about making a game is that it's not always just a simple series of steps. Games can become quite complex. As you become more confident in your programming skills, you can begin to think about the following:

* The characters in your game: What is the purpose of each character? What does each character do? How do the different characters interact with each other? What instructions will need to be given to the characters?

* The objects in your game: What is the purpose of each object? i.e. a golden star may be a reward to be found and collected that will boost a user's points. Do the objects have any particular uses?

* The gameplay environment: Are there multiple levels? How do you progress from one level to another? Do certain areas within the game environment trigger special activities?

QUICK EXPERT SUMMARY

TELL ME A JOKE

 ## ADDING SOURCE CODE

So, you've come up with your idea, done your flowchart and written your pseudo code. Now things start to get interesting. We're going to write a short program, which can tell us some jokes.

We've learnt a lot so far about working with Python and using the print function on the input and print lines. Now let's familiarise ourselves with the Python file editor (IDLE). If you have the IDLE open then you can simply select **File** and then **New File** to open the file editor window.

Did you know that Guido van Rossum named Python after Monty Python's Flying Circus, the smash hit British comedy show?

SAY WHAT?

Enter the following source code in the new file editor window:

```
1. print ('What did the spider do on the computer?')
2. input()
3. print ('Made a website')
4. input()
5. print('Why does the computer keep sneezing?')
```

```
6. input()
7. print('It has a virus!')
8. print()
9. print('What is a cow\'s favourite day?')
10. input()
11. print('Moo-year\'s Day')
12. print()
13. print('What do you call an underwater spy?')
14. input()
15. print('James Pond!')
16. print()
17. print('Knock Knock')
18. input()
19. print('Who\'s there?')
20. input()
21. print('Ashe')
22. input()
23. print('Ashe who?')
24. print('Bless you!')
25. print()
26. print('Knock Knock')
27. input()
28. print('Who\'s there?')
29. input()
30. print('Who')
31. input()
32. print('Who who?')
33. print('Is there an owl
    in there?')
```

Examine lines 1 to 4 in the source code. Because we don't want to reveal the punchline of the joke immediately, we have placed an input() function after the first line of the joke. At this stage the user can press the **Enter** key and it will reveal the next line of the joke or, if they wish, they can enter a string of text (such as: I don't know, what did the spider do on the computer?). However, because we haven't told the computer to store the text it will just forget it as we move on.

Now take a look at lines 9, 19 and 28. In each case you will find a backslash in the middle of the sentence. This has been done because we need an apostrophe in our sentence and in order for the computer to print it we must put a backslash in before it. When you run the code it will not print the backslash and you will see the sentence as normal. The backslash is known as an escape character.

In order to run your program, you can now press **F5** on your keyboard or select **Run** and then select **Run Module F5**.

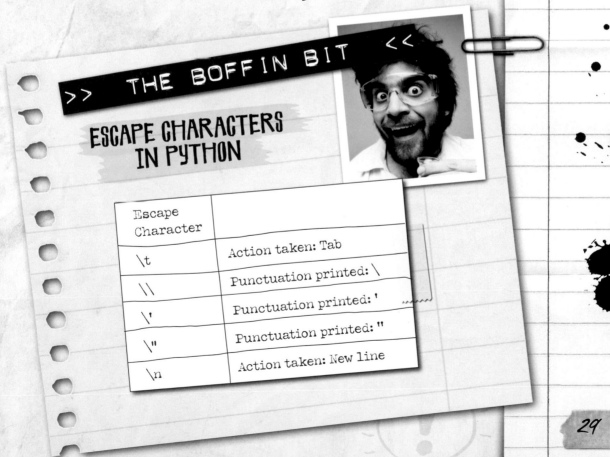

>> THE BOFFIN BIT <<

ESCAPE CHARACTERS IN PYTHON

Escape Character	
\t	Action taken: Tab
\\	Punctuation printed: \
\'	Punctuation printed: '
\"	Punctuation printed: "
\n	Action taken: New line

* PERSONALISE THE GAME

Can we extend the program? How could we adapt it in some way? Two simple adaptations can make the program more personal and interactive. The first would be to welcome the user with their own name and for the second we can ask them if they would like to read the Knock, Knock jokes or not. See pages 32—36 for a detailed explanation of the code.

The modified code would be:

```
1.    print('Hello, what is your name?')
2.    name=input()
3.    print('Hello', name, 'I hope you are well
      today. Let\'s make you laugh with a few
      jokes')
4.    print()
5.    answer='N'
6.    print ('What did the spider do on the
      computer?')
7.    input()
8.    print ('Made a website')
9.    print()
10.   print('Why does the computer keep sneezing?')
11.   input()
12.   print('It has a virus!')
13.   print()
14.   print('What is a cow\'s favourite day?')
15.   input()
16.   print('Moo-year\'s Day')
17.   print()
18.   print('What do you call an underwater spy?')
```

```
19.   input()
20.   print('James Pond!')
21.   print()
22.   print('Would you like to hear
      some Knock, Knock jokes now?
      enter Y for yes and N for no')
23.   answer=input()
24.   if answer=='Y' or answer=='y':
25.       print('Knock, Knock')
26.       input()
27.       print('Who\'s there?')
28.       input()
29.       print('Ashe')
30.       input()
31.       print('Ashe who?')
32.       print('Bless you!')
33.       print()
34.       print('Knock, Knock')
35.       input()
36.       print('Who\'s there?')
37.       input()
38.       print('Who')
39.       input()
40.       print('Who who?')
41.       print('Is there an owl in there?')
42.       print('That\'s the end, thank you
          ',name,' bye bye for now.')
43.   else:
44.   print ('Bye Bye', name, 'thank you for
      listening to my jokes')
```

31

Welcoming the user with a personal message

1. `print('Hello, what is your name?')`

2. `name=input()`

3. `print('Hello', name, 'I hope you are well today. Let\'s make you laugh with a few jokes')`

4. `print()`

5. `answer='N'`

So, the first line is pretty straightforward. It's a simple print line that asks the user their name. It's the second line that we need to consider. This line declares a variable called 'name' and sets its value to be whatever is entered by the user in response to the question on line 1. So, in this example, it will store the user's name as they enter it.

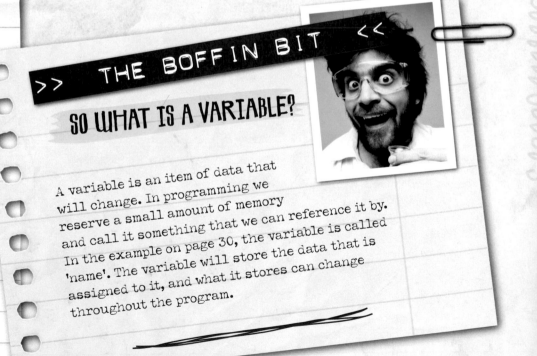

>> THE BOFFIN BIT <<

SO WHAT IS A VARIABLE?

A variable is an item of data that will change. In programming we reserve a small amount of memory and call it something that we can reference it by. In the example on page 30, the variable is called 'name'. The variable will store the data that is assigned to it, and what it stores can change throughout the program.

You will notice that the print command on line 3 is different from what you've been usually typing in. The apostrophes are used to break up the text string with the variable (' , name, ') referenced in between. Use commas to separate where a string section ends and where a variable is referenced.

Line 5 declares a variable called answer: answer = 'N'. It's standard practice to declare the variables that you will use at the start of your program. So, even though we won't actually need to use the answer variable until later, we have to mention it first. In Python when you declare variables you have to assign them some content to begin with. We are giving this variable a default value of 'N'.

Asking the user a question

Look back at our source code on pages 30–31. Lines 22–44 deal with the question: Would you like to hear some Knock, Knock jokes now? If the answer is yes, then the program will provide more jokes. If the answer is no, then the program will end. We can represent this in the following flowchart:

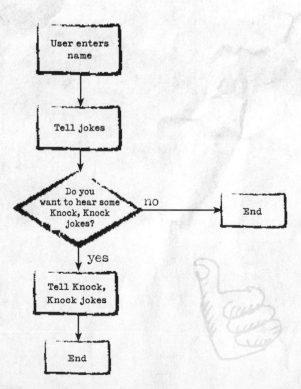

The diamond shape is known as a decision box. In programming it is usually represented as an IF statement. IF statements in programming allow the program to follow an alternative path. So, if the answer to a question is yes, one path is followed, if the answer to a question is no, a different path is followed. In our Tell Me a Joke program this is covered on lines 22–44.

The first part of this is to ask the user if they want to read any 'Knock, Knock' jokes, and then to store that answer in a variable. The code for this is:

```
22.    print('Would you like to hear some Knock,
       Knock jokes now? enter Y for yes and N for
       no')
23.    answer=input()
```

The variable called 'answer' will store whatever the user types in; this should be a Y or an N to represent the answers yes or no.

Line 24 then begins the IF statement.

```
24.    if answer=='Y' or answer=='y':
```

Note, the double '='. The equals sign is used once to assign a value, for example lines 2 and 5 in the code. When used twice it's almost like asking the question 'is it equal to?'. So, the IF statement above is really saying "IF [*the variable*] answer is equal to Y or [*the variable*] answer is equal to y then..." This will recognise the user's response as ' yes' whether they enter the letter 'y' in upper case or lower case.

Lines 43 and 44 simply print a goodbye message if the user enters 'N' instead.

DEBUGGING

No, we're not talking about pest control, well not exactly. Debugging is all about getting rid of those pesky bugs once and for all.

'Bugs' in programming refers to things that you've got wrong, perhaps a misplaced variable, a missing colon, too many brackets or instructions in the wrong order. Solving these errors is the act of debugging.

So, how do you debug? Quite often it's just a case of going through your code and rereading it, but here are a few tips to get you started:

1. When you want to test that your game works, choose **Run Module** or press **F5** from the IDLE. If there are errors, it will tell you.

2. Get hold of a volunteer and explain your program to them, what you're trying to do and why it's not working. Talking your problem through out loud helps you resolve issues in your own head.

3. If you're faced with a logical error, then these can be hard to pick out. So break down your program and deal with each part separately. Study your program against your original pseudo code – does it differ? Are things happening in the correct sequence?

4. The most common syntax errors are usually due to missing colons, incorrect indentation or capital letters in the wrong places. Python is very sensitive about these. Usually, when you run your program, Python will be able to identify quite a lot of the errors and tell you what it doesn't like.

Using indentations

After the IF statement, lines 25–42 are indented. These indentations are important in Python and if you forget to indent your code you will generate a syntax error. Indentation allows you to see where code 'belongs'. So, for example, once you've declared your IF statement the code below is indented to illustrate that it's part of that statement.

Now we've come to the end of your code and your Tell Me a Joke game is complete!

SAY WHAT?

Rumour has it that the term 'bug' came from the fact that one of the first errors in the operation of a computer arose because a moth became stuck amongst the components!

QUICK EXPERT SUMMARY

- Enter source code in Python to begin your program. Remember to use the escape characters for certain grammatical symbols.
- Use variables to store data that may change through the program. Remember to use apostrophes around the variable.
- Use IF statements when you want the user to follow an alternative path.

GUESS MY NUMBER

✳ OVERVIEW

Right, we're going to create a number-based game. The game is quite simple, but it has the potential to be modified to become quite complex. It's a number guessing game where the user plays against the computer. So, your top-down approach to this game would look something like this:

1. The computer generates a random number between 1 and 10

2. The user tries to 'guess' the number by inputting their own number

3. The computer responds by telling the user whether their guess was 'correct', 'too high' or 'too low'

4. The user wins the game by correctly guessing the computer's random number

5. At the end of the game the computer displays the number of attempts the user made to guess the number.

37

* FLOWCHART FOR GUESS MY NUMBER

We can use the top-down approach on page 37 to create a flowchart of the program. We want to add a simple personal element to the program. It would be great to welcome the user with their name and then use that later in the program as well.

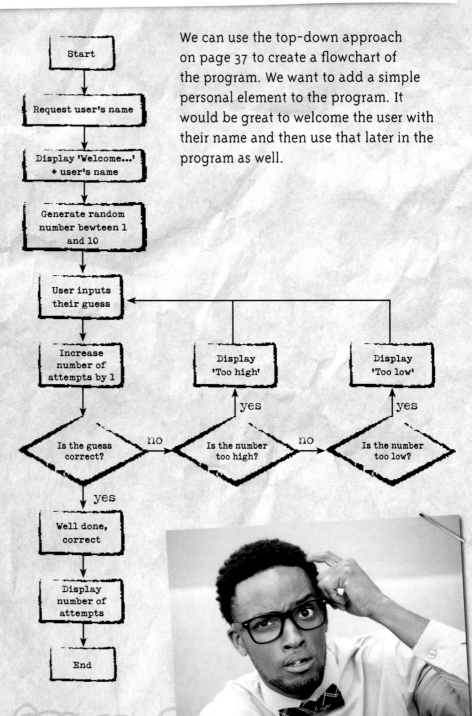

```
Start
  ↓
Request user's name
  ↓
Display 'Welcome...' + user's name
  ↓
Generate random number bewteen 1 and 10
  ↓
User inputs their guess
  ↓
Increase number of attempts by 1
  ↓
Is the guess correct? --no--> Is the number too high? --no--> Is the number too low?
      |yes                          |yes                            |yes
Well done, correct            Display 'Too high'             Display 'Too low'
  ↓
Display number of attempts
  ↓
End
```

✳ PSEUDO CODE FOR GUESS MY NUMBER

Now use the Guess My Number flowchart and convert it into pseudo code.

```
Print 'Hi, what's your name?'

Username variable = answer

Print 'Welcome...' + username

MyNumber variable = random number between 1 and 10

Print 'Enter your guess'

UserGuess variable = answer

Attempts variable = attempts + 1

Repeat until UserGuess = MyGuess

If UserGuess = MyGuess   then

Print 'Well done' + Username + 'you correctly
guessed the answer in', Attempts, 'attempt'

Else

If UserGuess > MyGuess then

Print 'Too high'

Else

Print 'Too low'
```

* SOURCE CODE FOR GUESS MY NUMBER

Take a look at the source code below. Read it through before you attempt to copy it out. Can you work out what it's doing and how it works?

1. Import random **#Imports a module that deals with random numbers**

2. No2Guess=random.randint (1,20) **#Generates a random number between the upper and lower number**

3. print ('I have guessed a number between 1 and 20. Can you work out what it is?')

4. **#Initialise a variable called 'turn', this will increment to keep track of the number of turns**

5. turn = 1

6. **#Takes variable 'guess' and assigns it the value entered by the user**

7. guess = int(input ("Enter your guess, you have 10 attempts"))

8. **#Begin the loop – 'range (10)' gives the user 10 attempts**

9. for loopCounter in range (10):

10.   if guess == No2Guess: **#Does the user's entry match the computer's number?**

11.   print ('Congratulations, you won!')

12.   print ('You won in', turn, 'tries')

13.   **#Adds number of attempts to message**

14.   break

15.   **#Close the loop**

16.   elif guess > No2Guess: **#Otherwise, is the user's entry higher?**

17.   print ('Too high')

18.   guess = int(input("Enter another guess"))

19.   turn +=1 **#Increment the number of attempts by 1**

```
20.  elif guess < No2Guess: #Otherwise, is the
     number too low?
21.  print ('Too low')
22.  guess = int(input("Enter another guess"))
23.  turn +=1 #Increment the number of attempts
     by 1
```

Using the Random module

Now it's time to get your programming goggles on and take a look at the first line of the source code:

```
Import random #Imports a module that deals
with random numbers
```

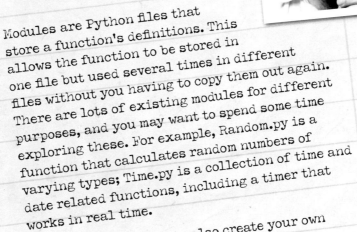

>> THE BOFFIN BIT <<

WHAT IS A MODULE?

Modules are Python files that store a function's definitions. This allows the function to be stored in one file but used several times in different files without you having to copy them out again. There are lots of existing modules for different purposes, and you may want to spend some time exploring these. For example, Random.py is a function that calculates random numbers of varying types; Time.py is a collection of time and date related functions, including a timer that works in real time.

It is possible for you to also create your own modules. Since Python is open source, many developers have continued to create their own modules and then made them freely available. A popular example of this is the module PyGame. PyGame allows you to add graphics to your games.

Hmmm, did somebody just say pie?

https://www.pygame.org

Random is a module in Python that deals with random numbers. By simply writing 'import random' we are importing the entire Random module and all the functions contained within it. When you wish to use a function from within a module, you will need to reference the name of the module before you write the name of the function: No2Guess = random.randint(1,20). A variable called No2Guess has been declared. We want this to store the computer's randomly generated number. So we assign to it a random number and use a function that we've imported from the random module: randint. Randint is a function from within the Random module that gives us a random number, anywhere from 1 to 20.

Setting a variable

```
print ('I have guessed a number between 1 and 20.
Can you work out what it is?')
```

```
turn = 1
```

The third line prints out your introductory message. The fifth line declares a variable called turn (this will store the number of attempts made by the user) and sets the initial value at 1. Usually variables have an initial value of 0, especially if they are being used as counters. However, we know that each player will have at least one attempt, so we can set the variable to 1 here.

Converting string to whole numbers

```
guess = int(input("enter your guess, you have 10
attempts"))
```

In the seventh line, 'guess' stores the user's suggested number. The next part of the code creates an input prompt i.e. this is where the computer asks the question and then waits for an answer from the user. The message displayed to the user is written in the quotation marks, and the computer waits until the user has provided an answer and hit enter, before it moves on to execute the next instruction in your program. So far, so good.

❝ Great coders are today's rock stars. ❞

will.i.am

However, because by default this form of input recognises data as 'string' (i.e. text) the computer will not be able to do numerical comparisons with it. Therefore, the text needs to be recognised as a number, and that is what the function int() does. int() is a built-in instruction that deals with whole numbers (integers). We can use it to convert the text into a numerical value. In this case, the numerical value is the user's guess. It is possible to separate this code out onto separate lines, but, for efficiency, we can simply incorporate it into one line.

Loop and IF statement

The ninth line of your source code (page 40) reads:

```
for loopCounter in range (10)
```

This creates a loop, which runs for a limited number of attempts. (Have you gone loopy yet?) In this case, the user has a maximum of 10 attempts. Try varying the number in the brackets. You can make the game more difficult, by limiting the number of guesses to 5, or make it easier by increasing it to 15 or 20.

```
if guess == No2Guess:
        print ('Congratulations, you won!')
        print ('You won in', turn, 'tries')
```

Now we begin the section of code that allows the computer to work out whether the user's guess was correct, too high or too low. The first part of this code sets the criteria for the IF statement (see page 34). Here, we are simply asking if the guess entered by the user is the same as the number generated by the computer.

The indented code below will be triggered if the answer is yes. So, when the number guessed by the user matches the number generated by the computer, the user has won the game. A congratulations message will be printed, along with a record of the number of attempts they made. The 'break' command at the end closes and exits the user from the loop.

```
elif guess > No2Guess:
print ('Too high')
guess = int(input("Enter another guess"))
turn +=1
```

The elif command means 'else if...'. So, if the criteria is false, then the number will be checked to see if it's too high or too low. In this instance, we can check to see if the guess made by the user is higher than the computer's number. If this is the case, then an appropriate message will be given to the user, telling them that it's too high. They will then be prompted to enter another guess. The turn +=1 line simply adds the value '1' to the number already in the variable called 'turns'. Therefore, recording the number of attempts made to guess the number.

```
elif guess < No2Guess:
print ('Too low')
guess = int(input("Enter another guess"))
turn +=1
```

This is the final criteria of the IF statement: if the number guessed is neither correct or too high, a comparison is made to check if the number of guesses is too low. Users are given another attempt and the number of attempts made is recorded.

DIY DUDE

Modifying the game

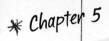

Dude!

Below are possible modifications that you can make to your game:

1. Welcome each player individually

2. The user plays against another player

3. The game doesn't end automatically when the answer is guessed correctly; instead it repeats, allowing multiple 'plays' until the user doesn't want to play any more.

Try to make the suggested modifications yourself. Remember, write out your pseudo code before you start creating your solution. This will make the process much easier.

Modification 1:

For this you are likely to need an additional variable to store the username. This username is then used as part of the welcome string to welcome the user. Since the username is stored as a variable, it can also be called back again at the end for a personalised goodbye message.

Modification 2:

Decide how you want a second player to interact. If the first player suggests a number for the second to guess, you may need to rethink quite a lot of the structure of your game. For example, by default, whatever number the first user enters will appear on screen. The game is no fun if the second user can see the answer before they begin!

Perhaps both players could take turns guessing? Again, you will still need to continue to use a selection of variables, loops and IF statements.

Modification 3:

You will have to build in a feature where the user is asked if they wish to continue. What will follow this will probably be an IF statement that examines the user's answer and recognises whether or not they wish to continue.

You've already used the 'FOR' loop (see page 44) which loops until a counter reaches a certain number. There is also a 'While' loop (see page 54). This allows you to set a condition. For example, the syntax structure for this would be:

```
variable = 'x'
while variable == 'x':
        do these steps….
```

QUICK EXPERT SUMMARY

- Modules usually contain functions of a certain type or theme. Python has several that have been pre-developed.

- Use the Random function to automatically generate a random whole number between an upper and lower limit.

- Convert text (string) to whole numbers (integers) in order to do calculations.

- Use a loop when you need a set of instructions to repeat several times.

- Use an IF statement within another IF statement when you want to compare against more than one criteria.

WIZARDS AND KINGDOMS

CREATE A ROLE-PLAY GAME

Are you ready to add a touch of magic to your next program? You're going to create a game called Wizards and Kingdoms. This is a text-based game, which will allow the user to choose a path to increase their magical powers, or fail and face a curse instead! Creating this game will allow you to introduce several new programming concepts.

✳ PLANNING WIZARDS AND KINGDOMS

So, how will the game work? Let's stick to the first level of the game and start by planning that. Then you can use the principles to expand the game however you wish. Using our previous method, list the major steps and functions (the algorithm) first:

1. The player is exploring and travelling the magical lands

2. Wizards live in towers; some are good and some are bad

3. Bad wizards will cast a curse on the player and turn them into a frog

4. Good wizards will increase the player's magical powers

5. The game starts and the player is faced with two towers

6. The player chooses a number and enters the corresponding tower

7. A random function will allocate a tower with a good or bad wizard

8. Once a player encounters a wizard the game ends and the player either wins (if they meet a good wizard) or loses (if they meet a bad wizard).

As before, you can illustrate the algorithm for this game using a flowchart. The flowchart for this game could look similar to the one below:

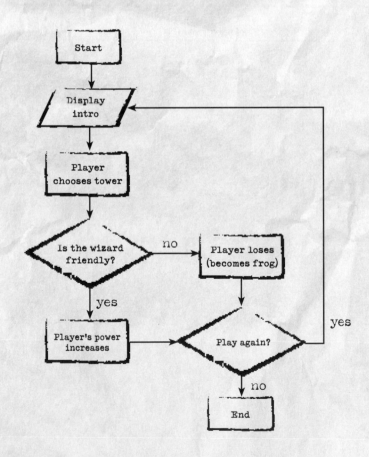

Now that you have sorted out the algorithm for your new game, you'll need to write out some pseudo code for it. Have a go at writing out some pseudo code for yourself, it will help you clarify exactly how your game is going to work.

✳ PROGRAMMING WIZARDS AND KINGDOMS

Take a look at the source code below. Examine it and see if you can work out what all the separate elements are doing, as it is important to understand what you are inputting and why. Copy out the source code to build your game. Don't forget to test it to see if it works, and feel free to modify it and change it as you go along.

```
1.  #Import random and time modules
2.  import random, time
3.  #Function which displays introductory text to
    set the scene
4.  def Introduction():
5.      print('You are a trainee wizard in a
        magical kingdom and you want to increase your
        magical strength.')
6.      print('In front of you, you see two tall
        towers. In one tower the wizard is friendly')
7.      print('and will increase your magical powers.
        In the other')
8.      print('the wizard is evil, and he will turn
        you into a frog on sight.')
```

```
9.    print()
```

10. **#This function stores the user's choice for the tower they wish to enter**

```
11. def whichtower():
12.    tower = ''
13.    while tower!='1' and tower!='2':
14.        print('Which tower do you want to enter? (1 or 2)')
15.        tower = input()
16.    return tower
```

17. **#This function sets the scene for the chosen tower and will randomly assign the chosen tower a good or bad wizard**

```
18. def checktower(chosentower):
19.    print('You approach the tower...')
20.    time.sleep(2) #Sets a 2 second delay between one message and the next
21.    print('It is tall and dark...')
22.    time.sleep(2)
23.    print('An old and imposing wizard suddenly appears in front of you, and...')
24.    print()
25.    time.sleep(2)
26.    nicewizard = random.randint(1, 2) #Randomly assigns value 1 or 2 to variable
```

27. **#The if statement below checks to see if the chosen tower is the same as the value assigned to the nice wizard**

28. #If they are the same then player's magical power is increased, otherwise a curse is given and the player loses

29.   if chosentower == str(nicewizard):

30.   print('...increases your magical powers.')

31.   else:

32.   print('...waves his wand and in a flash turns you into a FROG!')

33.   return chosentower

34. #This is the main block of code which uses and calls all previous functions declared

35. playagain = 'yes'

36. while playagain == 'yes' or playagain=='y':

37.   Introduction()

38.   towernumber = whichtower()

39. #A new variable stores the results of the function whichtower

40.   checktower(towernumber)

41.   print('Do you want to play again? (yes or no)')

42.   playagain = input()

✳ EXAMINING WIZARDS AND KINGDOMS

It's time to go through the code that makes up the Wizards and Kingdoms game bit-by-bit, so that you can clearly understand each section of the game. Then you can use your creative talents to develop this game further and decide what happens next...

Import modules

#Import random and time modules

import random, time

So, the first two lines of code we've seen before and actually they are pretty straightforward. Remember, the hashtag denotes an explanatory note to explain your code. The second line simply imports the modules (see page 42) that contain the functions associated with random numbers and time.

The function

```
#Function which displays introductory text to
set the scene
def Introduction():
    print('You are a trainee wizard in a
    magical kingdom and you want to increase your
    magical strength.')
    print('In front of you, you see two tall
    towers. In one tower the wizard is friendly')
    print('and will increase your magical powers.
    In the other')
    print('the wizard is evil, and he will turn
    you into a frog on sight.')
    print()
```

This function is very simple. It contains no parameters and it simply displays the introductory text for the game. Not all functions have to carry out calculations. This one simply contains a lot of text. The final print command contains no text, and it is simply to provide a blank line in the code before the next prompt appears.

Use a loop

```
#This function stores the user's choice for the
tower they wish to enter
def whichtower():
    tower = ''
    while tower!='1' and tower!='2':
        print('Which tower do you want to enter?
        (1 or 2)')
        tower = input()
    return tower
```

So, the next function simply deals with the user's choice of which tower they wish to enter. The value they enter is stored in a variable called tower. Can you work out why the code is being dealt with in this way? The while command initiates a loop (this type of loop is known as the While loop) which will continue to operate *while* the given criteria is true. What does this mean? Run your code and when prompted to choose a tower to enter, try entering a number that *isn't* 1 or 2. See what happens… The code becomes stuck in the loop *until* you enter the value 1 or 2. The moment you do, it continues with the game.

Time for another function...

```
#This function sets the scene for the chosen
tower and will randomly assign the chosen tower
a good or bad wizard

def checktower(chosentower):

    print('You approach the tower...')

    time.sleep(2) #Sets a 2 second delay between
    one message and the next

    print('It is tall and dark...')

    time.sleep(2)

    print('An old and imposing wizard suddenly
    appears in front of you, and...')

    print()

    time.sleep(2)

    nicewizard = random.randint(1, 2) #Randomly
    assigns value 1 or 2 to variable

#The IF statement below checks to see if the
chosen tower is the same as the value assigned
to the nice wizard

#If they are the same then a new spell is
granted, otherwise a curse is given and the
player loses

    if chosentower == str(nicewizard):

        print('...increases your magical
        powers.')

    else:

        print('...waves his wand and in
        a flash turns you into a FROG!')

    return chosentower
```

The checktower function is probably one of the most important and complex functions within this game. It actually does several things. You will have noticed that the first set of 'print' commands are separated by the command 'time.sleep(2)'. The sleep function has been imported from the time module and simply adds a two-second delay in between messages that appear on the screen. If you use the 'time.sleep(2)' command, the user doesn't have to do anything and the next line will automatically appear after the set time delay (measured in seconds).

nicewizard is a local variable declared, which is a variable that can only be used within the function. It has one job, to store the random number (1 or 2). This will be the number given to our good wizard. If it matches the number of the tower chosen by our user, then they will be granted increased magical powers.

Then, the IF statement simply checks if the tower chosen by the user (1 or 2) is the same as the value assigned to our nice wizard (1 or 2). If the two match then a new spell is granted, if they don't then the user is cursed to spend their life as a frog!

Pulling it all together

```
#This is the main block of code which uses and
calls all previous functions declared
playagain = 'yes'
while playagain == 'yes' or playagain=='y':
        Introduction()
        towernumber = whichtower()
#A new variable stores the results of the
function whichtower
        checktower(towernumber)
        print('Do you want to play again? (yes or
        no)')
        playagain = input()
```

This is the final block of code in our program. It calls together all the previous functions and decides when and how they should be used. So, we have declared a variable called 'playagain' and given it a default value of 'yes'. While this condition remains true, the game will continue to run.

The game begins by setting the scene and displaying the introductory lines. The next line calls the whichtower function and assigns the value generated to a variable called towernumber. This is then used in the checktower function to see if the wizard is a good or bad one. The result of whether the player has won or lost is also generated by this function. The game ends by asking whether or not the user wishes to play again. If they enter anything other than 'y' or 'yes' then the game ends.

✳ CAN YOU SEE THE STRUCTURE?

Can you see how the functions that you have defined have been used to break down the game into separate parts? Each element of the game has its own function and this allows it to be dealt with separately. Programming in this way helps you to organise the game and your code. Organised code is much easier to debug (see page 35) and modify. It follows a set structure, and using this structured approach can make programming much easier.

✳ WHAT NEXT?

Now that you've mastered the world of programming you can move on to create bigger and better games... There is a lot more to programming and Python than has been covered in this book. Thanks to the wealth of modules that you can import and use within Python, the possibilities are endless.

https://docs.python.org/2/
library/turtle.html

https://trinket.io/python/
bbe92df381

Do you remember using Logo? Your maths teacher may have used it with you to teach you angles. Well, think Logo and combine it with the power of Python... it leads to some interesting results. You can import the 'Turtle' module into Python. Try using the site Trinket; they've created an interactive Python application for the web that uses Turtle graphics. You can even customise the code in your web browser, or just copy and paste it into the IDLE on your computer.

It's a given that games usually have a heavy graphical element to them. However, none of the games mentioned in the previous chapters have included any graphics. Why? Well developing games is essentially a combination of good programming, artwork and storytelling. The games you play today wouldn't exist without some complicated programming running behind the scenes. That's why the three programs you've developed in the previous chapters all focus on the programming rather than the graphics. Once you have mastered the programming, implementing the graphical side should become a piece of cake!

So, how can you create beautifully illustrated games? Pygame is a free open source module that adds sound, graphics and animation functionality to Python.

Try importing the 'tkinter' module into Python. The tkinter module provides you with everything you need to create a Graphical User Interface for your program. Soon your program will look more like the software that you use on your computer desktops.

http://pygame.org/download.shtml

DIY DUDE
Adding graphics and illustrations

Dude!

QUICK EXPERT SUMMARY

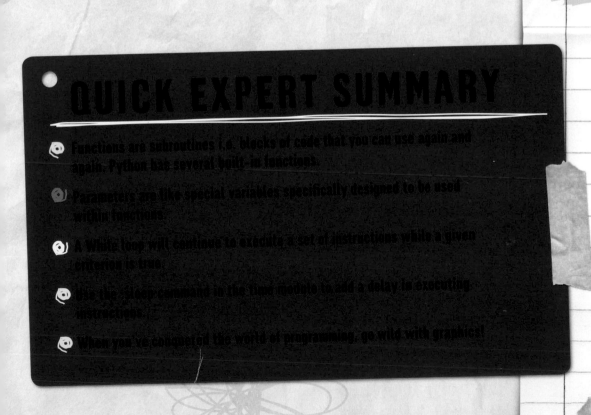

- Functions are subroutines i.e. blocks of code that you can use again and again. Python has several built-in functions.

- Parameters are like special variables specifically designed to be used within functions.

- A While loop will continue to execute a set of instructions while a given criterion is true.

- Use the 'sleep' command in the 'time' module to add a delay in executing instructions.

- When you've conquered the world of programming, go wild with graphics!

THE LAST WORD ON BEING A PROGRAMMER

Having **dipped your toe** in the water of programming, hopefully you can now **go forth** and create your own **successful computer program**. The most important thing to remember is to **have fun!**

>> USEFUL LINKS <<

✳ **GOOGLE'S PYTHON CLASS**
https://developers.google.com/edu/python/

✳ **GUIDO (THE INVENTOR OF PYTHON) LETTER TO YOUNG PROGRAMMERS (AND HIS BLOG)**
http://neopythonic.blogspot.com.au/2013/10/letter-to-young-programmer.html

✳ **INVENT WITH PYTHON**
http://inventwithpython.com/chapters/

✳ **PYGAME**
http://pygame.org/

✳ **PYTHON 4 KIDS**
http://python4kids.wordpress.com/

✳ **PYTHON DOCS — TURTLE LIBRARY**
https://docs.python.org/2/library/turtle.html

✳ **TRINKET — INTERACTIVE PYTHON ON THE WEB**
https://trinket.io/python/bbe92df381

✳ **YOUTUBE: COMPILERS VS INTERPRETERS**
https://www.youtube.com/watch?v=_C5AHaS1mOA&feature=youtu.be

✳ **YOUTUBE: USING PYTHON THE SHELL AND THE IDLE**
https://www.youtube.com/watch?v=kXbpB5_ywDw

Algorithm – a series of steps/instructions taken to solve a problem.

Command line interface – also known as a console user interface (CLI). It is a means of interacting with the computer where the user issues a series of written commands to the program. The response generated by the program is also often text based.

Comments – comments are used in programming to help explain key sections of the code. Single-line comments begin with a '#' so that the computer knows not to compile these as code.

Computational thinking – a set of skills and techniques for solving problems. It is based around five key themes: algorithmic thinking, evaluation, generalisation, abstraction and decomposition.

Conditional branches – a sequence of code that is executed only when certain criteria have been met. Conditional branches are often implemented through something known as selection statements or IF statements.

Escape character – A character that causes subsequent characters to be given an alternative interpretation. A common escape character in programming is the backslash.

Functions – a sequence of programmed instructions that perform a specific task.

These are self-contained and can be used within other programs wherever that task needs to be performed.

Graphical User Interface – a method of interacting with the computer visually using graphics to represent icons, windows and menus.

IDLE – (Integrated Development Environment) a Windows-based environment that allows you to write and debug Python code.

IF statements – used to provide alternative routes within programs. An IF statement will choose which series of instructions to execute depending on whether or not a given criterion is true.

Iteration – the repetition of a process in programming. This is also referred to as a loop.

Logical errors – the bugs in a program that cause it to operate incorrectly; for example, through calling an incorrect subroutine. The syntax may be correct and therefore the program will not crash.

Loops – repeating a sequence of instructions within a loop. There are different types of loops; for example, within Python a 'FOR' loop will repeat the sequence of instructions for a set number of times. However, the 'WHILE' loop will continue to repeat a sequence of instructions *while* a given criteria is true.

Module — a file containing function definitions and statements. A module remains independent but can be imported into any program for the use of its functions.

Operator — single/multiple characters that may behave similar to functions. Each operator will represent an action. For example, the '+' denotes addition while the '*' commonly denotes multiplication.

Parameters — special types of variable used as part of a subroutine/function. These are also referred to as arguments and they provide the data to be input into the subroutine when it is being used.

Pseudo code — an informal high-level description of an algorithm or computer program. It follows the normal constructs of a programming language but it is designed to be read and understood by humans rather than machines.

Selection statements — will select and execute a given set of instructions depending on whether or not a given criterion is true.

Shell — the Python interpreter. Writing your program in the Python shell will result in each line of code being executed as you input it.

Source code — a set of commands ready to be compiled into an executable computer program.

String — a data type that refers to a sequence of characters; also referred to as 'text'.

Structured programming approach — this is a programming paradigm that uses subroutines and a block-like structure to improve the clarity and development time of a computer program.

Subroutine — a self-contained sequence of instructions that are designed to specifically perform a frequently used task.

Syntax — the structure of statements within a computer programming language.

Variable — a name given to identify a storage location for a small piece of data. The values held within variables are likely to change through the course of the program.

>>> INDEX <<<